For [God's Words] are life to **Andrew**, they are healing and health to **his** entire body.

- Proverbs 4:22

Andrew's

healing

SCRIPTURES

MyVersion LLC.

Andrew's Healing Scriptures

Print Edition
ISBN 13: 978-1-5429-2671-3
Copyright © 2017 MyVersion LLC.

All Scripture quotations are translated directly out of the Hebrew and Greek. Most scriptures in this book are slightly and carefully modified to fit the tense, person, and voice of the sentence. Also, some contextual words may be added in to clarify the meaning of a passage. NOTE: Special care was taken to ensure the original meaning of the passage was not changed in any way.

All scriptures marked KJV are taken from the King James Version of the Bible

Printed in the United States of America.

Published by MyVersion LLC.
For more information visit: http://MyVersion.org
email: info@MyVersion.org or call 408-MY-BIBLE

Contents

at
that
to our

g healed and
scriptures over
thing mystical or
how faith works.
that faith comes by
by the Word of God.
urself speaking the Word
rises up and accesses the
esus made available when he
cross for you.

ii

Our heavenly Father has an important work for each of us in the body of Christ to do. It will require a strong, healthy body with totally healed members. That's why we all need to walk in complete health.

Speaking His Word about our health is wh... keeps us healed! Proverbs 4:22 says God's Words are healing and health... bodies. That is powerful!

See Andrew, the key to stayin... whole is speaking healing... yourself. This is not some... magical. This is just... Romans 10:17 says... hearing and hearin... When you hear y... of God, faith... healing that... died on the...

This book is broken up into two sections, one containing the promises from the Old Covenant (Old Testament) and the other containing your realities in the New Covenant (New Testament). The entire Bible is inspired by God and is useful for teaching (2 Timothy 3:16) so as New Testament believers, we can stand on God's Word both in the Old and New Testament.

As you read through this book, take ownership of the Scriptures you read and speak them over yourself as reality in your life. Faith will rise up, and you will see big changes in your body and life.

Andrew's Promises from the Old Covenant

If **Andrew** will diligently listen and obey the voice of the Lord **his** God and will do what is right in His sight, and will listen to and obey His commandments and keep all His statutes, God will not allow any of the diseases upon **Andrew** which were brought upon the Egyptians, for God is the Lord Who heals **Andrew**.

- Exodus 15:26

When **Andrew** serves the Lord **his** God; the Lord will bless **Andrew's** food and water, and the Lord will take away all sickness from **Andrew's** body.

- *Exodus* 23:25

The Lord will protect **Andrew** from all sickness and disease, He won't let **Andrew** suffer from all of the terrible diseases of Egypt.

- *Deuteronomy* 7:15

If **Andrew** will diligently listen to the voice of the Lord **his** God, being watchful and alert to do all the commandments which He commands **him** today, the Lord God will set **Andrew** high above all the nations of the earth. And all these blessings shall come upon **Andrew** and overtake **him** if **he** heeds the voice of the Lord **his** God.

- Deuteronomy 28:1-2

I, the Lord, call heaven and earth to witness the choice that **Andrew** will make today. I have set before **Andrew** life and death, blessings and curses; therefore choose life, that **Andrew** and **his** descendants may live and may love the Lord God, obey His voice, and cling to Him. For He is **Andrew's** life and the length of **his** days, that **Andrew** may dwell in the land which the Lord swore to give to **his** fathers, to Abraham, Isaac, and Jacob.

- Deuteronomy 30:19-20

Every single good and perfect promise that the LORD has given **Andrew** has come true.

- Joshua 21:45

Praise the Lord who has given rest to **Andrew**, just as he promised. Not one word has failed of all the wonderful promises He gave to his servant **Andrew**.

- 1 Kings 8:56

"My covenant with **Andrew** will I not break, nor will I alter the thing that is gone out of my lips.

— Psalm 89:34

"With long life will I satisfy **Andrew** and show **him** My salvation.

— Psalm 91:16

"I am the Lord who forgives every one of **Andrew's** iniquities, Who heals each one of **Andrew's** diseases.

— Psalm 103:3

He brought them forth also with silver and gold: and there was not one feeble person among their tribes.

- Psalm 105:37

He sent out His word and healed **Andrew**, snatching **him** from the door of death.

- Psalm 107:20

Andrew shall not die; instead, **he** will live to declare the works and recount the illustrious acts of the Lord.

- Psalm 118:17

Andrew must trust in the Lord with all **his** heart, and not rely on **his** own understanding. In all **his** ways **Andrew** must acknowledge Him, and the Lord will make **his** paths smooth.

- Proverbs 3:5-6

Andrew must pay attention to my words; consent and submit to my sayings. **he** must not let them leave **his** sight; **he** should let them penetrate deep into the center of his heart. For they are life to **Andrew**, healing and health to **his** flesh. Also, **Andrew** must keep and guard **his** heart with all vigilance, for it determines the course of **his** life.

- *Proverbs* 4:20-23

Fear not [there is nothing to fear], for I, the Lord, is with **Andrew**; do not look around in terror and be discouraged, for I am **Andrew's** God. I will strengthen and harden **Andrew** to difficulties, yes, I will help **him**; yes, I will hold **Andrew** up and retain **him** with My victorious right hand of righteousness and justice. For I the Lord your God hold **Andrew's** right hand; I am the Lord, Who says to **Andrew**, "Fear not; I will help you!"

- *Isaiah* 41:10;13

I, even I the Lord, am He Who blots out and cancels **Andrew's** transgressions, for My own sake, and I will not remember **Andrew's** sins. **Andrew,** put Me in remembrance [remind Me of **Andrew's** merits]; let us plead and argue together. Set forth **Andrew's** case, that **he** may be justified (proved right).

- Isaiah 43:25-26

Surely the Lord has borne **Andrew's** weaknesses (sicknesses, griefs, and distresses) and carried **his** sorrows and pains, yet they ignorantly considered Him stricken, smitten, and afflicted by God. But He was w o u n d e d f o r **A n d r e w's** transgressions, He was bruised for **Andrew's** guilt and iniquities; the chastisement needed to obtain peace and well-being was upon Him, and with the stripes [that wounded] Him, **Andrew** is healed and made whole.

- *Isaiah* 53:4-5

Then the Lord said to **Andrew**, "You have seen well, for I am alert and active, watching over My Word to perform it."

- *Jeremiah* 1:12

For I, the Lord, will restore health to **Andrew**, and I will heal **his** wounds, says the Lord, because they have called **Andrew** an outcast, saying, This is **Andrew**, whom no one seeks after and for whom no one cares!

- *Jeremiah* 30:17

Beat your plowshares into swords, and your pruning hooks into spears; let the weak say, I am a strong warrior!

- *Joel* 3:10

The Lord is so good, A strength and stronghold in the day of trouble; He knows, cares for, and understands **Andrew**, when **he** takes refuge and trust in Him. Whatever plot the enemy devises against the Lord, He will make a complete end of it; affliction [of **Andrew**] will not occur twice.

- Nahum 1:7-9

Andrew's

Realities

in the

New Covenant

And behold, a leper approached Jesus and, laying on his face, worshiped Him, saying, Lord, if You are willing, You are able to cleanse me and make me whole. And Jesus reached out His hand and touched him, saying, I am willing; be cleansed and cured. And instantly his leprosy was cured and cleansed.

- Matthew 8:2-3

And Jesus fulfilled what was spoken by the prophet Isaiah, He Himself took in order to carry away **Andrew's** weaknesses and infirmities and carried away **Andrew's** diseases.

- Matthew 8:17

"Truly I tell you, whatever **Andrew** forbids and declares to be improper and unlawful on earth must be what is already forbidden in heaven, and whatever **Andrew** permits and declares proper and lawful on earth must be what is already permitted in heaven. Again I tell you, if **Andrew** and another on earth agree (harmonize together, make a symphony together) about whatever [anything and everything] they may ask, it will come to pass and be done for them by My Father in heaven. For wherever two or three are gathered in My name, there I AM in the midst of them.

- *Matthew* 18:18-20

"...If **Andrew** has faith and does not doubt, **he** will not only do what has been done to the fig tree, but even if **Andrew** says to this mountain, Be taken up and cast into the sea, it will be done.

- Matthew 21:21

"**Andrew** will pick up serpents; and [even] if **he** drinks anything deadly, it will not hurt **him**; **Andrew** will lay **his** hands on the sick, and they will get well and recover.

- Mark 16:18

Behold! I have given **Andrew** authority and power to trample upon serpents and scorpions, and [physical and mental strength and ability] over all the power that the enemy [possesses]; and nothing shall in any way harm **Andrew**.

- *Luke* 10:19

We know that God does not listen to sinners; but if **Andrew** is God-fearing and a worshiper of Him and does His will, God listens to **him**.

- *John* 9:31

The thief comes only in order to steal and kill and destroy. I came that **Andrew** may have and enjoy life, and have it in abundance (to the full, till it overflows)- *John* 10:10

Abraham did not weaken in faith when he considered the impotence of his own body, which was as good as dead because he was about a hundred years old, or when he considered the barrenness of Sarah's deadened womb. Just like Abraham, No unbelief or distrust makes **Andrew** waver or doubtingly question concerning the promise of God, but **he** grows strong and is empowered by faith as **he** gives praise and glory to God, Fully satisfied and assured that God is able and mighty to keep His word and to do what He had promised.

- Romans 4:19-21

And if the Spirit of Him who raised up Jesus from the dead dwells in **Andrew**, then He Who raised up Christ Jesus from the dead will also restore to life **Andrew's** mortal body through the Holy Spirit who dwells in **him**.

– Romans 8:11

For as many as are the promises of God to **Andrew**, they all find their Yes [answer] in Christ. For this reason we also utter "Amen" (so be it) to God through Him to the glory of God.

– 1 Corinthians 1:20

" Christ purchased **Andrew's** freedom, redeeming **him** from the curse of the Law and its condemnation by Himself becoming a curse for **Andrew**, for it is written, cursed is everyone who hangs on a tree (is crucified);

- *Galatians* 3:13

" And I am convinced and sure of this very thing, that He Who began a good work in **Andrew** will continue it until the return of Jesus Christ, developing that good work and perfecting and bringing it to full completion in **him**.

- *Philippians* 1:6

Not in **Andrew's** own strength for it is God who is all the while effectually at work in **Andrew** energizing and creating in **him** the power and desire, both to will and to do for His good pleasure, satisfaction and delight.

- *Philippians* 2:13

Andrew must not fret or have any anxiety about anything, but in every circumstance and in everything, by prayer and petition (definite requests), with thanksgiving, **Andrew** will continue to make **his** wants known to God. And God's peace will be **Andrew's**, [that tranquil state of a soul assured of its salvation through Christ, and so fearing nothing from God and being content with its earthly lot of whatever sort that is, that peace] which transcends all understanding shall garrison and mount guard over **Andrew's** heart and mind in Christ Jesus. For the rest; whatever is true, whatever is worthy of reverence and is honorable and seemly, whatever is just, whatever is pure, whatever is lovely and lovable, whatever is kind and gracious, if there is any virtue and excellence, if there is anything worthy of praise, **Andrew** will think on, weigh, and take account of these things [fix **his** mind on them].

- *Philippians* 4:6-8

Let **Andrew** seize, hold fast, and retain without wavering the hope **he** cherishes and confesses, for He Who promised is reliable and faithful to His word.

- *Hebrews* 10:23

Andrew must not fling away **his** fearless confidence, for it carries a great and glorious compensation of reward.

- *Hebrews* 10:35

Now faith is the assurance (title deed, confirmation) of things **Andrew** hopes for (divinely guaranteed), and the evidence of things **Andrew** can't see [the conviction of their reality—faith comprehends as fact what cannot be experienced by the physical senses].

- Hebrews 11:1

Jesus Christ (the Messiah) is [always] the same, yesterday, today, and forever (to the end of the age).

- Hebrews 13:8

If **Andrew** is deficient in wisdom, **he** should ask of the giving God who gives to everyone liberally and ungrudgingly, without reproaching or faultfinding, and it will be given to **him**.

— James 1:5

So be subject to God. When **Andrew** resists the devil and stands firm against him, he will flee from **him**. As **Andrew** comes close to God, He will come close to **Andrew**.

— James 4:7

Is **Andrew** sick? **he** should call on the church elders (the spiritual guides). And they should pray over **him**, anointing **him** with oil in the Lord's name. And the prayer of faith will save (heal, set free, deliver) **Andrew**, and the Lord will restore **him**; and if **he** has committed sins, **he** will be forgiven.

- James 5:14-15

Jesus personally bore **Andrew's** sins in His own body on the tree as on an altar and offered Himself on it, that **Andrew** might die to sin and live to righteousness. By His wounds and lashes **Andrew** has been healed.

- 1 Peter 2:24

Andrew must cast the whole of **his** care [all **his** anxieties, all **his** worries, all **his** concerns, once and for all] on Jesus, for He cares for **Andrew** affectionately and cares about **him** watchfully. **Andrew** must be well balanced (temperate, sober of mind), vigilant and cautious at all times; for **his** enemy, the devil, roams around like a lion roaring in fierce hunger, seeking someone to seize upon and devour. **Andrew** must withstand him; be firm in faith, knowing that the same (identical) sufferings are appointed to the whole body of Christians throughout the world.

- 1 Peter 5:7-9

And, beloved, if **Andrew's** conscience (**his** heart) does not accuse **him** [if it does not make **him** feel guilty and condemn **him**], **Andrew** has confidence before God,   And **Andrew** receives from Him whatever **he** asks, because **he** [watchfully] obeys God's orders [observe His suggestions and injunctions, follow His plan for **him**] and practices what is pleasing to Him.

- 1 John 3:21-22

And this is the confidence (the assurance, the privilege of boldness) which **Andrew** has in the Lord: that if **he** asks anything (makes any request) according to His will (in agreement with His own plan), He listens to and hears **him**. And since **Andrew** knows that God listens to **him** in whatever **he** asks, **he** also knows that **he** has the requests made of Him.

- 1 John 5:14-15

I pray that **Andrew** may prosper in every way and that **his** body may keep well, even as I know **his** soul keeps well and prospers.

- 3 John 1:2

And **Andrew** has overcome (conquered) the enemy by means of the blood of the Lamb and by the speaking of **his** testimony...

- *Revelation* 12:11

A Prayer For Healing

Listen Andrew, if you are ready to receive healing today, or if you just want to release your faith for health and wholeness, you can receive right now. Jesus is your healer! You just read that throughout this whole book! Your part is to say and do. Say out loud, "Jesus is MY healer. He bore my sicknesses and my diseases and pain. I expect to receive now!"

Speak the following prayer in faith and mean it with your whole heart. Accept it and believe it!

Father, the Word of God that I have heard and confessed is the power of God unto salvation. I confess Jesus Christ as Lord over my life—spirit, soul and body. I receive the power of God to make me whole, sound, delivered, saved and healed now. I act on the Word of God and receive His power.

Sickness, disease and pain, I command you to go in the Name of Jesus. You are not the will of God for me. I enforce the Word of God on you. I will not tolerate you in my life. Leave my presence! I will never allow you back.

I have been healed and made sound. Jesus made me whole. My days of sickness and disease are over.

I am the saved. I am the healed. The power of sickness over my life has been broken forever. Jesus bore my sicknesses. Jesus bore my weakness. Jesus bore my pain— and I am free.